THE WAY
OF THE LAMB

THE WAY
OF THE LAMB

CHRIST IN THE APOCALYPSE

Lenten meditations

HANS-RUEDI WEBER

BOOK SERIES

WCC Publications, Geneva

Cover design: Rob Lucas

ISBN 2-8254-0918-9

© 1988 WCC Publications, World Council of Churches,
150, route de Ferney, 1211 Geneva 20, Switzerland

No. 36 in the Risk book series

Printed in Switzerland

Table of contents

Introduction

John's Revelation is visual theology. It must be *seen* in order to be understood. The visions are accompanied by sounds: cries of pain and joy, the thunder of storms and the rumbling of earthquakes, the hymns of multitudes and the oracles of divine messengers. To what is seen corresponds an oral theology which has to be *heard* and must be recited with a loud voice.

Writing a *book* about John's Revelation risks, therefore, the danger of alienating with the print medium a message which originally has such a strongly visual and oral character. John took this same risk when he wrote down the visions and oracles which he received. However, what he wrote became a manuscript, a unique original document written by hand, and not a mass-produced book.

Moreover, in the old days such manuscripts were read aloud and memorized, and thus functioned immediately again as an oral tradition. Later, when the manuscripts of John's Revelation were copied down and passed from one generation to the next, copyists gradually illuminated them with miniatures, so that the essentially visual character of the message was recovered.

This booklet is meant to become a help for liturgical celebrations. Chapters 2-4 are in fact expanded versions of a series of Holy Week meditations, given in April 1987 in the chapel of the Ecumenical Centre in Geneva, Switzerland. Corporate reading of the text, music, art meditation, prayer, sung liturgical responses, spoken comments: all these are necessary to recapture something of what John saw and heard and what he wanted to communicate. Even those who read this booklet privately should recite aloud the texts from Revelation, take sufficient time to let the art work speak to them and join in the singing of the hymns and responses.

The visions and oracles which John received are not easy to understand. They do not have the narrative quality which makes the gospel stories so attractive. Nor do we find here the kind of theological reasoning which we have in Paul's letters, drawing the readers into a corporate search for truth. Instead we are faced with a bafflingly quick change of scenes and symbols. If one turns to commentaries and special essays on John's Revelation the confusion becomes even greater because of the divergent and often contradictory interpretations proposed.

While preparing these meditations there came a time when it seemed right to put aside for a while such learned studies. I recorded the whole of John's Revelation on a cassette and repeatedly listened to this less than 90 minutes recording. Instead of stopping again and again and trying to figure out what this or that symbol, this or that sudden change of scene and mood signified, I let the whole of the theo-poetic message penetrate me and make its impact on my mind and imagination.

This does not mean that now I understand it all. There are still many passages of Revelation which continue to puzzle and even irritate me, some of which I find myself wishing that John had never written. Nonetheless, the liturgical drama of this cosmic exodus story and the power of its visions, poetry and hymns have gripped and worked within me.

The warnings and encouragements which the seer John conveyed, around 95 A.D., to the Christians in Asia Minor can still speak to us today. They squarely face the realities of contemporary power struggles and confront them with the power of God as it manifested itself in the death and resurrection of Christ. They also open up a wide horizon of time and space. All things and all people must pass through the fire of judgment, but within and beyond the sufferings in church and world history there is the promise of a new heaven and a new earth.

The meditations in this booklet concentrate on a few passages which deal with Christ the Lamb. These texts must be seen within the framework of the whole of John's Revelation.

The following division into various parts is certainly not the only possible one, but it does indicate the main acts of the drama. After the commissioning and the greetings (Rev. 1:1-8) John receives his first vision and he addresses letters of warning and encouragement from Christ to the seven churches in Asia Minor (1:9-3:22). Then the seer is taken up into heaven where in a liturgical context the key event of history is disclosed to him (4:1-5:14). Subsequently he receives three cycles of visions, those about the seven seals, the seven trumpets and the seven bowls (6:1-8:1; 8:2-11:19; 15:1-16:21). These do not point to three subsequent stages in history, but they are like a spiral, always referring to the same centre and the same goal of history. An enigmatic revelation about the woman robed with the sun, the red dragon with the two beasts and the Lamb with his followers (12:1-14:20) links the sevenfold vision of the trumpets to that of the bowls. The latter is expanded by the description of the fall of Babylon and the announcement of the wedding feast of the Lamb (17:1-19:10). This leads to the return of Christ and the events which conclude world history (19:11-20:15). The culmination of all is the last great biblical parable of God's kingdom: the vision of the new Jerusalem and the river of living water (21:1-22:5). The book then ends with a threefold Epilogue (22:6-21).

Three further comments might help us in our understanding of John's Revelation:

— The last book of the Bible is a re-reading of the Old Testament in the light of Christ. No other writing in the New Testament has as many references to a wide range of Old Testament texts and concepts (more than half of its verses contain one or more of such references). In the following meditations it will not be possible to identify this for every passage discussed, but the use of a good biblical study guide can help readers discover the rich Old Testament background of John's Revelation.

— It is not by chance that John received his visions on the "Lord's Day", on a Sunday when in his exile on Patmos he felt a special spiritual communion with the churches worshipping on that day. The Book of Revelation comes out of the milieu of worship and it can be best understood in the context of a worshipping community.

— An equally important context for discovering the message of John's Revelation is the struggles of faith of Christians in the world. The first addressees were divided and deeply disturbed local churches who began to face persecutions and who were full of doubts. Was the death of Christ really the decisive victory in God's drama of salvation? Is the Lamb's way indeed the way to true life? Yes, answers John the prophet and witness from his exile in Patmos. He calls for a spirituality of resistance, confronting the worship of idols, especially the emperor cult, with the true worship of God.

This booklet is dedicated to the Worship Committee of the Ecumenical Centre in Geneva and its present moderator Lynda who in her wheelchair is a source of songs, courage and hope.

H.R.W.

1. The Song of Moses and of the Lamb

"They were singing a new song."

In the last book of the Bible we hear much singing. The most appropriate way of entering a meditation on John's Revelation is therefore to sing a new song.

YOU ARE HOLY

I and II can be sung at the same time in two different groups.

Moses took off his shoes when he came to the burning bush in the desert of Sinai. He was standing on holy ground. John, the seer of Patmos, fell down as though dead when he heard the voice of the crucified and risen Christ. Both Moses and John felt that they were in the presence of God. This same sense of divine presence fills all those who meditate on what is testified in the Book of

Revelation. To sing the above song thus expresses well
the basic attitude and convictions mediated to us by the
Apocalypse. John himself describes what he experienced
on a Sunday during his exile:

*"I, John, your brother and partner in hardships, in the
kingdom and in perseverance in Jesus, was on the island
of Patmos on account of the Word of God and of witness to
Jesus; it was the Lord's Day and I was in ecstasy, and I
heard a loud voice behind me, like the sound of a
trumpet... I turned round to see who was speaking to
me... When I saw him, I fell at his feet as though dead, but
he laid his right hand on me and said, 'Do not be afraid; it
is I, the First and the Last; I am the Living One, I was
dead and look — I am alive for ever and ever, and I hold
the keys of death and Hades. Now write down all that you
see of present happenings and what is still to come.'"*

(1:9-19)

John had to pass through the experience of death and
resurrection in order to become a true witness. This
points, like a parable, to the central message of the
Revelation. What it points to is life: the life of Christ, the
life of God's servants, ultimately even the life of the
whole of God's creation. However, no direct way leads
from what is now to what is to come. Life can be gained
only through a crisis. Just as Christ had to pass through
death and resurrection so God's servants must pass
through suffering, some even through martyrdom. There
is no new creation without the crisis of judgment.

During his initial vision John saw Christ with the eyes
of the prophet Daniel, as "a Son of Man" (compare Rev.
1:13-16 with Dan. 7:9-14; 10:5f.). This is one of the many
ways in which Christ appears in the Book of Revelation.
There are other, more typical manifestations by which the
crucified and risen Lord showed himself to the seer; for
instance those found in the initial greeting. The messages
which John sent to the seven churches come "from Jesus

Christ, the faithful witness, the First-born from the dead, the highest of earthly kings" (1:5). However, by far the most frequent description of Christ in the last book of the Bible is that of "the Lamb".

This designation must not immediately be identified with the Lamb of God found in other books of the New Testament (in Greek *ho amnos*, John 1:29,26; Acts 8:32; 1 Pet. 1:18). In John's Revelation another Greek term is used, *to arnion*, which can be translated both as "lamb" and as "ram". It occurs once in the Gospels (John 21:15) and once it designates a false prophet in the form of a beast "who had two horns like a lamb" (Rev. 13:11). In all 28 remaining passages *to arnion* refers to the Christ of the Apocalypse. These references are in chapters 5:6,8,12,13; 6:1,16; 7:9,10,14,17; 12:11; 13:8; 14:1,4,10; 15:3; twice in 17:4; 19:7,9; 21:9,14,22,23,27 and 22:1,13.

One could hardly find a better visual summary of John's Revelation than that on the medieval ivory tablet from the cathedral treasury of Tournai in Belgium (Plate 1). The unknown artist may have not consciously thought of what John saw and heard. Nevertheless, what he portrayed is indeed the Christ of the Apocalypse.

The lower part of the tablet shows the crucifixion of Jesus which became the decisive victory in the struggle with the forces of darkness. The sun and the moon to the left and right above the cross indicate that what happened at Golgotha has cosmic significance. Under the cross stands the figure of the Ecclesia with the cup, the church receiving Christ's blood for the eucharist. The person on the other side is less easily identifiable. Similar representations sometimes place opposite the Ecclesia the figure of the Synagogue. Here, however, the second person under the cross represents more likely the personified city of Jerusalem who looks up to the expected Messiah, her bridegroom. This parallelism between God's church and the New Jerusalem is indeed strongly emphasized in the Book of Revelation.

On the upper part of the tablet the risen Christ sits enthroned and makes a majestic gesture with his right hand. In his left hand he holds a book with the inscription *Salus Mundi* — "Salvation of the world". Christ is the Alpha (A) and the Omega (Ω) of world history, as these first and last letters of the Greek alphabet indicate to the right and left of Christ's head. Two angels and the "four living creatures" worship the enthroned Lord. These creatures originally symbolized God's power over the whole creation, but from the third century A.D. onwards they became the symbols of the four evangelists.

In the centre of the tablet a large circle formed by acanthus leaves attracts the attention. Within it two angels hold up a smaller circle in which stands the Lamb. As already indicated and as will be shown in the course of these meditations the figure of the Lamb sums up the particular testimony of John the seer. It recalls and combines three different Old Testament figures: in the first place the Passover lamb whose blood preserved the Israelites from destruction and thus made possible their exodus from slavery (Ex. 12:21-23); then the suffering Servant of God who was "like a lamb led to the slaughter-house" (Isa. 53:7); and lastly the Davidic Messiah described as a servant Shepherd (Ez. 34:23).

Looking at the ivory tablet from Tournai can introduce us to the world of imagery found in the last book of the Bible. Similarly, hearing the Song of Moses and of the Lamb can open our understanding for the special context and message of John's Revelation.

John: *I saw in heaven another sign, great and wonderful: seven angels were bringing the seven plagues that are the last of all, because they exhaust the fury of God. I seemed to be looking at a sea of crystal suffused with fire, and standing by the lake of glass, those who had fought against the beast and won, and against his statue and the number which is his name. They all had harps from God, and they were singing the hymn of Moses, the servant of God, and the hymn of the Lamb:*

All: *How great and wonderful are all your works, Lord God Almighty; upright and true are all your ways, King of nations. Who does not revere and glorify your name, O Lord? For you alone are holy, and all nations will come and adore you for the many acts of saving justice you have shown."*

(15:1-4)

This passage forms the introduction to the seven plagues caused by the seven bowls of God's fury. We are here immediately confronted with the dark side of John's Revelation, with the judgment of God. Those who feel too righteous and despise this world may enjoy such thunder-and-fire passages in apocalyptic literature. Many others feel ill at ease. Is this the God of steadfast love and enduring faithfulness whom we meet in so many parts of the Old Testament? Is this the God who became incarnate in Jesus Christ? Nevertheless, this dark side of what John saw and heard cannot be ignored and we will still have to face the anger of God and of the Lamb.

It is significant, however, that like all other visions of judgment on earth so also the one beginning in the fifteenth chapter starts in heaven with music and singing. Those for whom the Book of Revelation was written — the churches now in the midst of the struggles of faith on earth — are told that a multitude of faithful have already passed the test. They endured and remained loyal to Christ (14:12). They have "fought against the beast and won, and against his statue and the number which is his name". The Greek text says literally: "They won the victory *out of* the beast", out of the power realm of satanic forces. Here John points in a veiled way to the evil powers which counter God's purpose of salvation.

The question about the identity of the "beast" will never be fully solved. Throughout the centuries, the interpretation of chapters 12-14 has led to different and contradictory understandings. One thing is clear: in John's visions the great dragon (= Satan; 12:9) and the beast stand over against God and the Lamb. The "beast out of the sea" serves the dragon and it is helped in this task by a secondary "beast out of the earth", later identified with a false prophet. This prophet works in the disguise of a lamb. By its miracles he misleads people on the earth to worship the blaspheming primary beast, whose mysterious number is six hundred and sixty-six (13:1, 11-18).

Though it seems strange to modern minds, according to ancient number symbolism any of the following interpretations can be defended: six is opposed to the perfect number seven. The number 666, a repeated attempt to reach the perfect 7, may indicate that, despite its powers, persuasions and provisional victories, the struggle of the beast against God and the Lamb will for ever remain inconclusive and is doomed to defeat. In antiquity each letter also had a numerical value. The cipher 666 is thus the sum-total of the following words and designations which — among many others — have been suggested as possible decipherments: *thērion*, the Greek word for "beast"; "Nimrod", the mighty conqueror and founder of the Babylonian empire who would thus be seen as the type of all rebellious powers; "Caesar Neron" in Hebrew letters, recalling the ill-famed Roman emperor who ruled from 54 to 68 A.D. and whose persecutions of Christians in Rome had not yet been forgotten in the time of John the seer; various Greek abbreviations for the name and titles of the emperor "Domitian" who ruled from 81 to 96 A.D. and was considered by many as Nero reincarnated.

None of the above interpretations is totally convincing. The identity of the beast and the number of its name remain hidden as evil powers usually do. Most likely John and his addressees saw for their own time these powers incarnate in the new Nero, the emperor Domitian. This would explain also the warning not to worship the beast's "image" or "statue". Especially in Asia Minor Domitian strongly promoted the emperor worship by multiplying his image in statues and on coins.

Those who fought against the beast and won the victory now sing "the song of Moses and the song of the Lamb". In John's visions Moses and the Lamb are mentioned together only in this passage. Nevertheless, the link between the two figures provides a key for understanding the whole Book of Revelation: what formerly happened in the liberation of the Israelite tribes from slavery under the Pharaohs now happens on a cosmic scale. John's visions and oracles point to a universal exodus story. This is confirmed by other details in the text. There are the seven "plagues" (15:1, 8; 16:1-21), six of them resembling the plagues in Egypt (Ex. 7:17-12:34). The song is sung standing "by the sea of glass" (15:2; cp. 4:6). This probably forms the celestial counterpart to the Red Sea on whose shore Moses and Miriam sang their song of victory after having been saved from the pursuit of Pharaoh's army (Ex. 15). The "fire" in the sea may either be a reference to the test of suffering through which those who sing had to pass, or it is the reflection of God's glory in the heavenly sanctuary (Rev. 15:8). Another important symbol of the exodus story is mentioned in the same context: the "tent of the Testimony" (15:5).

The introduction to the new and last sevenfold vision of the trials before the end contains thus a typology which is much more revealing than all the speculations about the number 666. The "beast" becomes the antitype to Pharaoh, the "sea of glass" the antitype to the Red Sea, the "Lamb" the antitype to Moses, the universal exodus story the antitype for the first exodus story.

Can this parallelism be continued? To what extent is the song of the Lamb in Revelation 15 the antitype to the song of Moses in Exodus 15? Even today the latter plays an important part in the Sabbath evening service of the Jewish synagogue. Is Christian worship simply a parallel to and a continuation of Jewish worship?

Both the song of Moses and the song of the Lamb do not speak about human feats but concentrate on who God is and what God has done:

Yahweh, who is like you, majestic in sanctity,
who like you among the holy ones,
fearsome of deed, worker of wonders?...
In your faithful love you led out the people you had
*   redeemed,*
in your strength you have guided them to your holy
*   dwelling.*   *(Ex. 15:11,13)*

There are also some parallels to the other song of Moses, reported in Deuteronomy:

I shall proclaim the name of Yahweh.
Oh, tell the greatness of our God!
He is the Rock, his work is perfect,
for all his ways are equitable,
A trustworthy God who does no wrong,
he is the Honest, the Upright One! (Deut. 32:3f.).

Nevertheless, the tone of the song of the Lamb is strikingly different from that of the one sung by Moses, Miriam and the Israelites on the shore of the Red Sea. The latter sounds like a militant and passionate victory hymn, celebrating the triumph of God, the mighty warrior. To superficial readers such a triumphalistic song, both the one in Exodus and in Deuteronomy, would fit in well with the context of judgments reported in Revelation 14 and 16. However, those who through their endurance and faith are winning the victory over and out of the power realm of the beast do not sing a song of victory. No single word is said about their own sufferings or the judgment of the evil powers. The song of the Lamb only praises God, God's marvellous deeds and just ways, God's holiness which attracts all nations to come and worship in the divine presence.

It would be wrong to consider the Lamb and Moses or the New and the Old Testaments as being opposed to each other. In fact, with the exception of the last line, the whole of the song of the Lamb consists of quotations and allusions to Old Testament texts as the following list (which is far from complete) shows:

How great and wonderful are all your works
"You are great and do marvellous deeds" (Ps. 86:10). "How great are your works, Yahweh" (Ps. 92:5). "Great are the deeds of Yahweh" (Ps. 111:2). "All your works are wonders" (Ps. 139:14). "Sing a new song to Yahweh, for he has performed wonders" (Ps. 98:1).

Lord God Almighty (in Greek: "Pantokrator")
"Yahweh, God Almighty, is his name" (Amos 4:13 LXX).

Upright and true are all your ways
"All his ways are equitable. A trustworthy God who does no wrong, he is the Honest, the Upright One!" (Deut. 32:4). "Upright in all that he does, Yahweh acts only in faithful love" (Ps. 145:17).

King of nations: Who does not revere?
"Who would not revere you, King of nations?" (Jer. 10:7).

and glorify your name, O Lord?
    "All nations will... give glory to your name" (Ps. 86:9).
"My name is great among the nations" (Mal. 1:11).

For you alone are holy
    "You alone are God and Lord" (Dan. 3:45). "I, Yahweh
your God, am holy" (Lev. 19:2).

All nations shall come and adore you
    "All nations will come and adore you, Lord" (Ps. 86:9).
"Then all the nations will stream to it, many peoples will
come to it and say: Come, let us go up to the mountain of
Yahweh... that we may walk in his paths" (Isa. 2:2f.).
"To you the nations will come from the remotest parts of
the earth" (Jer. 16:19).

    Despite these many quotations from and allusions to
Old Testament texts in the hymn in the fifteenth chapter of
Revelation, the great differences with the Songs of Moses
in Exodus and Deuteronomy cannot be overlooked. These
songs celebrate not only the majesty of God, but also the
destruction of God's adversaries, be they the Pharaoh and
his armies, the disobedient Israelites or any other human
and cosmic power: "Yahweh is a warrior... Pharaoh's
chariots and army he has hurled into the sea"... "Hearing
of this, the peoples tremble" (Ex. 15:3ff., 14ff.). "Yes",
says Yahweh to the people of Israel, "a fire has blazed
from my anger, it will burn right down to the depths of
Sheol; it will devour the earth and all its produce... I shall
hurl disasters on them, on them I shall use up all my
arrows." "When I have whetted my flashing sword, I shall
enforce justice, I shall return vengeance to my foes"
(Deut. 32:22f.,41). No such vengeful notes appear in the
New Testament Song of Moses and the Lamb. Here the
ultimate outcome beyond all the judgments is envisaged;
the time when all will be made new is anticipated. The
nations shall then indeed walk on God's ways. In the

Greek original seven times the affirmation "no more" is proclaimed: the sea (the place from which the demonic powers come) will be no more, neither death, nor mourning, nor crying, nor pain. Even the night will be no more nor anything that is accursed. The nations will walk in the light of God's glory and the stream of the water of life will flow from the throne of God and the Lamb (Rev. 21:1-22:5).

It is from this perspective of the new creation that the whole Book of Revelation, including its dark sides, can most appropriately be understood. When reflecting on the self-giving of the Lamb, we shall in the next meditation discover still a second point in history and space from which John views what happens now on earth and what is still to come.

Prayer

Lord, we know how strongly the powers of darkness have invaded our lives and the structures of our societies. Nevertheless we believe that all nations will ultimately walk in your light. Therefore we dare to pray:

Grandchamp Community

Come splen-dour of God, in - vade all our dark - ness,

en - ligh - ten our hearts and re - main with your world

Lord, we confess that we ourselves often worship idols and help the powers of darkness. Judge us and help us to trust your steadfast love. Hear our prayer:

"Come splendour of God…"

Lord, how great and marvellous are all your works. Upright and true are all your ways. All nations will come and adore you, when you will make all things new. Answer our plea:
   "Come splendour of God…"

2. The Lion as the Lamb

Holy, Holy, Holy! Lord God Almighty!
Early in the morning our song shall rise to thee;
Holy, Holy, Holy! Merciful and mighty,
God in three Persons, blessed Trinity!

Holy, Holy, Holy! all the saints adore thee,
casting down their golden crowns around
    the glassy sea,
Cherubim and seraphim falling down before thee,
who wert and art, and evermore shalt be.

Holy, Holy, Holy! though the darkness hide thee,
though the eye of sinful man thy glory may not see,
only thou are holy, there is none beside thee
perfect in power, in love and purity.

Holy, Holy, Holy! Lord God Almighty!
All thy works shall praise thy name in earth
    and sky and sea;
Holy, Holy, Holy! merciful and mighty!
God in three Persons, blessed Trinity.

This famous early nineteenth-century hymn by Reginald Heber expresses well what John heard, saw and felt, when he was lifted up into heaven. The tune by J.B. Dykes with which these words are usually sung can be found in many hymnals.

There are two ways of receiving apocalyptic insight. The seer dreams and has visions whose significance an interpreting angel explains. Instances of this can be found in the Book of Daniel. Alternatively, the seer is taken up into heaven. There he hears and sees revelations which a heavenly interpreter explains as the meaning of what happens now on earth and what will happen in the future. John's Revelation is of this second type, as the seer himself explains:

"Then, in my vision, I saw a door open in heaven and heard the same voice speaking to me, the voice like a

trumpet, saying, 'Come up here: I will show you what is to
take place in the future.' With that, I fell into ecstasy and I
saw a throne standing in heaven, and the One who was
sitting on the throne, and the One sitting there looked like
a diamond and a ruby. There was a rainbow encircling
the throne…" (4:1-3)

A rainbow! The sign of God's promise for times when
things fall apart, when the world appears to disintegrate.

As John was lifted up into the presence of God his eyes
were blinded by the splendour he saw. His ears were
deafened by what he heard. He could not describe God,
the One sitting on the throne, for "flashes of lightning
were coming from the throne, and the sound of peals of
thunder" (4:5). Then his eyes began to focus: he saw
around God's throne twenty-four other thrones in a circle,
on which a heavenly senate sits, the twenty-four elders,
dressed in white robes. Like kings they wear crowns of
gold. Later it is said that they play harps and hold in their
hands, like priests, golden bowls full of incense. Perhaps
these angelic figures symbolize the twenty-four classes of
priests in the Old Testament. Or they represent the
outstanding leaders of the twelve tribes of Israel united
with the celestial church of the twelve apostles.

Nearer the throne John saw the "four living creatures",
heavenly beings similar to those whom the prophets Isaiah
and Ezekiel had seen in their visions (Isa. 6; Ez. 1). They
convey some idea of God's power over the whole
creation. The primary task of the whole assembly around
the throne is worship. Day and night John heard them sing
the "Sanctus":

Holy, Holy, Holy
is the Lord God, the Almighty;
who was, and is and is to come.

In the prologue to his Revelation the seer had
pronounced a beatitude: "Blessed is anyone who reads

(aloud) the words of this prophecy, and blessed those who hear them, if they treasure the content" (1:3). It is good to take this blessing seriously. What we have in the Book of Revelation are messages to be recited with a loud voice in order to be heard. Moreover, John describes in the fifth chapter the heavenly liturgy so vividly that it calls for a reading with different voices. The whole of this chapter must first make its impact on us. No need therefore to puzzle immediately about strange details such as the seven horns and seven eyes of the Lamb; they symbolize that the Lamb shares the power and knowledge of God. Towards the end of the reading three choirs will appear. First comes the one of the twenty-four elders. Then myriads of angels sing, as on the day when Jesus was born in Bethlehem (Luke 2:13f.). Finally a mighty cosmic choir appears, "everything that lives in heaven, and on earth, and under the earth, and in the sea". We will join these three choirs by reading aloud, letting the "praise and honour, glory and power" sound like the voice of the whole cosmos and joining also in the final "Amen!"

John: *I saw that in the right hand of the One sitting on the throne there was a scroll that was written on back and front and was sealed with seven seals. Then I saw a powerful angel who called with a loud voice:*

Angel: *"Who is worthy to open the scroll and break its seals?"*

John: *But there was no one, in heaven or on the earth or under the earth, who was able to open the scroll and read it. I wept bitterly because nobody could be found to open the scroll and read it, but one of the elders said to me:*

Elder: *"Do not weep. Look, the Lion of the tribe of Judah, the Root of David, has triumphed, and so he will open the scroll and its seven seals."*

John: *Then I saw, in the middle of the throne with its four living creatures and the circle of the elders, a Lamb that seemed to have been sacrificed; it had seven horns, and it had seven eyes, which are the seven spirits that God has sent out over the whole world. The Lamb came forward to take the scroll from the right hand of the One sitting on the throne, and when he took it, the four living creatures prostrated themselves before him and with them the twenty-four elders; each one of them was holding a harp and had a golden bowl full of incense which are the prayers of the saints. They sang a new hymn:*

All: *"You are worthy to take the scroll
and to break its seals,
because you were sacrificed, and with your blood
you bought people for God
of every race, language, people and nation
and made them a line of kings and priests for God,
to rule the world."*

John: *In my vision, I heard the sound of an immense number of angels gathered round the throne and the living creatures and the elders; there were ten thousand times ten thousand of them and thousands upon thousands, loudly chanting:*

All: *"Worthy is the Lamb that was sacrificed
to receive power, riches, wisdom,
strength, honour, glory and blessing."*

John: *Then I heard all the living things in creation — everything that lives in heaven, and on earth, and under the earth, and in the sea, crying:*

All: *"To the One seated on the throne and to the
Lamb,
be all praise, honour, glory and power,
for ever and ever."*

John: *And the four living creatures said:*
All: *"Amen."*

John: *And the elders prostrated themselves to worship.*

(5:1-14)

John weeps. In the Bible men also weep. This is one of the many distinguishing features which make the biblical message so truly human. John weeps because nobody is worthy to open the seals.

We can only guess what the content of this precious scroll might be. Some believe that God held in his right hand the Old Testament whose meaning could be rightly understood only when it is read in the light of Christ's death and resurrection. This was for instance the way in which a medieval artist interpreted the scroll (see page 19). More likely the document in God's hand symbolizes the divine will and design of salvation for the universe, perhaps best summarized in the title which John gave to his whole book: "Revelation (*apokalypsis*) of Jesus Christ" (1:1). The scroll is written on both sides so that nothing can be added. Does the double-sided script point to the fact that two different readings of what is now, what was and what will be are possible? This suggestion, made by one of the interpreters, is attractive, though it might not have been in the mind of the seer John. There would thus be an outer, superficial reading of world history and an "inside story", a reading which reveals and discloses the end and purpose of what happens in this time and cosmos.

However, the scroll is closed with seven seals. Nobody comes forward to take it and open the scroll. Nobody is worthy to reveal God's will. The inside story remains hidden and John bursts out in tears.

Then things begin to happen. John hears about the Lion of Judah, the new Davidic King. In the ancient blessing of Jacob, found in the book of Genesis, the tribe of Judah from whom both David and Jesus stem was likened to a lion:

"Judah is a lion's whelp...
Like a lion he crouches and lies down,
a mighty lion: who dare rouse him?

The sceptre shall not pass from Judah,
nor the ruler's staff from between his feet...
He washes his clothes in wine,
his robes in the blood of the grape" (Gen. 49:9-11).

In Christian iconography the lion can convey a whole range of meanings, from fierce evil forces to the highest royal majesty. If linked with the person of Christ the lion points to the power of resurrection. This goes back to the "Physiologus", an early Christian collection of legendary information about animals, plants and stones which are allegorically interpreted by references to biblical texts. The many translations and expanded versions of this popular booklet had a great influence on medieval art. In its first chapter the subject is the lion. Referring to Colossians 1:15 and Genesis 49:9 the unknown author there says: "When a lioness gives birth to her offspring, the whelp is born dead. She watches over the body until the lion comes on the third day. He breathes on the lifeless cub and restores life to it. Thus on the third day our almighty God, the Father of all, has raised from death his first-born Son, Jesus Christ our Lord. How appropriately Jacob said: 'Like a lion he crouches, like a lion's whelp he sleeps. Who shall wake him?'"

The lion's resuscitating power is often portrayed in medieval art. Thus a late thirteenth-century stained glass window (Fig. a) shows the lion's mighty breath bestowing life to the dead. In John's vision the image of the victorious lion gives way to another image: "I saw a Lamb (standing upright) that seemed to have been sacrificed" (5:6). The engraving on a cross from ca. 1100 A.D. captures well what John saw (Fig. b). Because Christ the Lamb was ready to give his life-blood, streaming into the communion cup, he is worthy to receive and open the scroll. God's hand appears now with a gesture of blessing.

Very seldom are Christ the Lion and Christ the Lamb portrayed together in Christian art. One of these rare

instances is a miniature in the early medieval Vivian Bible
(Plate 2). The upper half shows the Lion and the Lamb on
either side of God's throne with the four living creatures in
the four corners. As usual in medieval art God's presence
on the throne is indicated only through symbols, for
instance by a cross or a dove, in this case by the book with
seven seals. The Lamb has just broken the first seal and
therefore the rider on a white horse (6:2) already appears.
In the lower part of this miniature the artist shows the
effects of the event in heaven for people on earth. Moses
sits on an earthly throne, a veil covering his face. He
could not therefore understand the will of God. With a
reference to Exodus 34:29ff. Paul had written to the
Corinthians: "Until this very day, the same veil remains
over the reading of the Old Testament: it is not lifted, for
only in Christ is it done away with" (2 Cor. 3:14). This is
exactly what the artist communicates: now the veil is
being lifted. Three of the four living creatures pull away
the veil from Moses' face while the fourth creature blows
the golden trumpet, announcing the Gospel. Now the true
meaning of the Old Testament, of God's will and purpose,
can be seen. The Lion who becomes the sacrificial Lamb
makes the hidden story known.

The Lion and the Lamb: these two must be seen
together, as the first transforms himself into the second,
the Lion becoming the Lamb. Here the whole mystery of
Good Friday and Easter is visually summed up.

At the end of our first meditation we saw how John
helps us to see what happens in history and creation from
the perspective of the coming new creation. The vision
recorded in the fifth chapter of Revelation adds a second
perspective. What happens now on earth and what is still
to come must also be understood in the light of the events
on Good Friday and Easter, from the perspective of
Christ's death and resurrection.

For John these two are intimately united. It almost appears as if Easter preceded Good Friday. The seer hears about the victorious Lion before he sees the Lamb, and according to the original Greek text John notices that the Lamb is standing upright before he becomes aware of the marks of sacrifice. The victory is won not after but through the self-giving death of Jesus. Easter thus begins with the passion, with the sacrifice of the Passover Lamb and with the vicarious suffering of the Servant of God.

This has deep implications for the way Christians deal with power, a question in which churches throughout the centuries have often erred, drifting away from the way of the Lamb.

On the one hand there is the temptation for Christians and Christian institutions to play the human power game. With a false triumphalism they often impose themselves and their message on others, be it through "holy wars", by dominion or by the pernicious power of hidden persuasion. This is not the way of the Lion of Judah who became the Lamb, pouring out his life-blood for the salvation of the world.

On the other hand Christians and Christian movements are tempted to narrow down the cosmic hope of the biblical faith. With a false humility they often romanticize weakness and poverty. Such an attitude can lead to a mediocre piety: the hope for the universe becomes then a privatized religion of saved souls while the Caesars of this world remain unchallenged. This too is not the way of the Lion of Judah who won the victory as the slaughtered Lamb.

John's Revelation can help us to see both these as aberrations. It can save us:
— from the proud illusion that there is a way to God's kingdom which avoids the way to the cross;
— from the weakness of faith which no longer dares to hope for a new heaven and a new earth.

A superficial reading of what happens in world history creates the impression that brutal forces win the victory. What makes headlines are military and economic powers, the slogans of propaganda and publicity, the ever-present power of death. However, those to whom the inside story has been revealed can now already join the hymn of praise which assigns these seven attributes to the Lamb:

"Worthy is the Lamb that was sacrificed
to receive power, riches, wisdom,
strength, honour, glory and blessing" (5:12).

In the final chorus of his oratorio the "Messiah" Georg Friedrich Händel brought together words from the three choirs in the fifth chapter of Revelation. His majestic music for these shouts of praise sum up well what John heard during the heavenly liturgy. A good conclusion for this meditation is therefore to listen to a recording of the climax of Händel's "Messiah" with its long drawn-out "Amen". The words of this final chorus are:

"Worthy is the Lamb that was Slain,
and has redeemed us to God by his Blood,
to receive Power, and Riches and Wisdom,
and Strength and Honour and Glory and Blessing.
Blessings and Honour, Glory and Power
be unto him, that sitteth upon the Throne
and unto the Lamb
for ever and ever.
Amen!"

3. The Anger of the Lamb

Largo solenelle

American Negro Folk Song.

Refrain :

My Lord, what a morn-ing, My Lord, what a morn-ing, My Lord, what a morn-ing, When the stars be-gin to fall.

Fine.

Solo molto marc.

You'll hear de trum-pet sound, To wake de na-tions un-der-ground, Look in my God's right hand When de stars be-gin to fall.

You'll hear de sin-ner moan, To wake de na-tions un-der-ground, Look in my God's right hand When de stars be-gin to fall.

D. C. al fine

You'll hear de Christians shout, To wake de nations underground,
Look in my God's right hand, When de stars begin to fall.
You'll hear the angels sing, To wake de nations underground,
Look in my God's right hand, When de stars begin to fall.

Refrain : My Lord, etc.

You'll hear my Jesus come, To wake de nations underground,
Look in my God's right hand, When de stars begin to fall.
His chariot wheels roll round, To wake de nations underground,
Look in my God's right hand, When de stars begin to fall.

Refrain : My Lord, etc.

The scene and the atmosphere are changing.

As John proceeds from the visions he received in heaven to what he now sees happening on earth we are suddenly torn away from the divine liturgy. The majestic choirs of G.F. Händel's "Messiah" grow faint and we hear the cry and face the awe of a Black Spiritual. It is not music composed for concert halls and cathedrals, but a song for those who desperately struggle for hope in a situation without hope. This Spiritual was originally sung by slaves.

The action is still initiated in heaven, but the visions show the repercussions on earth. As Christ the Lamb breaks one seal of the scroll after another, four horses appear with their riders. The martyrs cry out of the depth: "How long?" The powerful and mighty of the earth hide themselves in caves and mountain crags, for a cosmic catastrophe strikes, which John describes with striking images: a violent earthquake; the sun turning black; the moon becoming red as blood; the stars falling down on the earth as a mighty gale shakes the world. The sky vanishes like a scroll that is being rolled up; all mountains and islands are shaken from their places.

Before reading the sixth chapter it is important to recall once again the purpose of the Book of Revelation: it is an encouragement and a warning for Christians who face persecution, for believers who begin to doubt whether Christ has indeed won the decisive victory over the evil powers of this world. What John saw and heard is not a blueprint of history, a Greek drama which inexorably follows its course of destiny. Rather, the vision shows the true character of the forces now active in world history. Christ reveals them, for as the paschal Lamb and the Suffering Servant he alone is worthy to open the scroll. Because he has already subjected himself to the world's judgment, he is able to transform cosmic catastrophes into the birthpangs of a new heaven and a new earth.

Through the events celebrated during Holy Week the ultimate outcome of history has become certain. It still remains undecided, however, where we ourselves finally stand: with the witnesses to Christ's victory on the cross or with those who want to hide as they face the anger of the Lamb. In the following reading we should therefore join in both the pleading of Christ's witnesses and the anguished cry of the mighty world.

John: *Then, in my vision, I saw the Lamb break one of the seven seals, and I heard one of the four living creatures shout in a voice like thunder:*

Voice: *"Come!"*

John: *Immediately I saw a white horse appear, and its rider was holding a bow; he was given a victor's crown and he went away, to go from victory to victory.*

When he broke the second seal, I heard the second living creature shout:

Voice: *"Come!"*

John: *And out came another horse, bright red, and its rider was given this duty: to take away peace from the earth and set people killing each other. He was given a huge sword.*

When he broke the third seal, I heard the third living creature shout:

Voice: *"Come!"*

John: *Immediately I saw a black horse appear, and its rider was holding a pair of scales; and I seemed to hear a voice shout from among the four living creatures and say:*

Voice: *"A day's wages for a quart of corn, and a day's wages for three quarts of barley, but do not tamper with the oil or the wine."*

John: *When he broke the fourth seal, I heard the voice of the fourth living creature shout:*

Voice: *"Come!"*

John: *Immediately I saw another horse appear, deathly pale, and its rider was called Death, and Hades followed at its heels. They were given authority over a quarter of the earth, to kill by the sword, by famine, by plague and through wild beasts.*

When he broke the fifth seal, I saw underneath the altar the souls of all the people who had been killed on account of the Word of God, for witnessing to it. They shouted in a loud voice:

All: *"Holy, true Master, how much longer will you wait before you pass sentence and take vengeance for our death on the inhabitants of the earth?"*

John: *Each of them was given a white robe, and they were told to be patient a little longer, until the roll was completed of their fellow-servants and brothers who were still to be killed as they had been.*

In my vision, when he broke the sixth seal, there was a violent earthquake and the sun went as black as coarse sackcloth; the moon turned red as blood all over, and the stars of the sky fell onto the earth like figs dropping from a fig tree when a high wind shakes it; the sky disappeared like a scroll rolling up and all the mountains and islands were shaken from their places. Then all the kings of the earth, the governors and the commanders, the rich people and the men of influence, the whole population, slaves and citizens, hid in caverns and among the rocks of the mountains. They said to the mountains and the rocks:

All: *"Fall on us and hide us away from the One who sits on the throne and from the anger of the Lamb. For the Great Day of his anger has come, and who can face it?"*

(6:1-17)

Throughout the sixth chapter Christ the Lamb remains the primary subject. He opens, one after another, each of the six seals and after an interlude he will also open the seventh seal which triggers the sevenfold vision of the trumpets (8:1ff.).

In a rapid sequence four horses and riders are called forth. The meanings of the second, third and fourth symbolic appearances are not too difficult to decipher though one must never forget that symbols have several layers of meaning.

The rider on the bright red horse with a great sword points probably to perverted political power. While in Romans 13:4 the sword is given to the political authorities for safeguarding justice in the service of God, here the sword serves to take away peace from earth. It becomes an instrument of war.

The rider on the black horse holding a pair of scales probably refers to a corrupt and exploitative economic power. This figure controls the prices of what is bought and sold. While in normal times twelve quarts of corn and twice as much of barley could be bought for a day's wages, now the prices are set so high that hardly the bare minimum can be purchased.

The rider on the deadly pale horse is called Death, collecting the cruel booty of victims for Hades, the realm of the dead.

The powers of politics, economics and death are indeed the driving forces in world history. If brought under the authority of God they can serve the divine purpose of salvation. However, there are times when, because of human greed and foolishness, political and economic powers become like madly galloping horses and leave behind a dreadful harvest for death.

The cavalcade of horses is led by an enigmatic rider on a white horse. He holds a bow and is given a crown. He rides forth to go from victory to victory though there is no mention of arrows or of his doing violence to anybody. Is this the figure of the Anti-Christ in the disguise of Christ,

Plate 1
Crucifixion, adoration of the Lamb and Majestas Domini. Relief in ivory from Nicasius Diptychon, ca. 900. Cathedral of Tournai. (See pp.3f.)

Figure a
Lion raising his still-born offspring. Stained glass window from Ritterstiftskirche in Wimpfen, 1270-1280. (See p.18.)

Figure b
Agnus Dei with hand of God, scroll and communion cup. Engraving on relic cross from Enger, ca. 1100. Berlin. (See p.18.)

Plate 2

*Lion and Lamb near the throne of God and the unveiling of Moses.
Miniature from Vivian Bible, St Martin in Tours, 846. (See p.19.)*

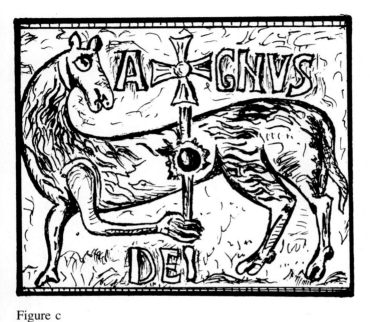

Figure c

Agnus Dei with cross staff. Lid of relic shrine, donated by the Esturian King Alfons the Great (866-910). Cathedral of Astorga. (See p.28.)

Plate 3
Lion with cross staff. Liber floridus, 1250-1270. Paris. (See p.28.)

Plate 4
*Lamb on Mount Sion. Miniature from Beatus of Burgo de Osma, 1086.
Cathedral of Burgo de Osma. (See pp.38f.)*

Plate 5

Agnus Dei with rivers of Paradise. Engraving of pierced copper plate gilded with gold, ca. 1160. Paris. (See pp.49f.)

Plate 6
Mosaics in sanctuary in San Vitale, ca. 537. Ravenna. (See pp.53ff.)

the King of kings who according to the nineteenth chapter will come to conclude human history? The false prophet also imitates Christ by appearing in the form of a lamb (13:11). Or is this first figure identical with that other rider on a white horse who clearly represents Christ (19:11-16)? Both interpretations have been defended by outstanding exegetes. Can the vocation of the first rider — "to go from victory to victory" — help discover his identity? "To win victory" (*nikān*) is indeed a key term in John's Revelation, but the seventeen passages where this verb occurs do not lead to any clear conclusion. On the one hand, the beast will and does indeed win victories over Christ's witnesses (11:7; 13:7). On the other hand it is clearly stated that the Lion of Judah has already won the victory (5:5), that the Christ is already victorious and will further defeat his opponents (3:21; 17:14). John also testifies that by the blood of the Lamb Christ's witnesses have won the victory (12:11) and are thus enabled to be victorious (seven times in chapters 2 and 3; 15:2; 21:7).

To see in the first rider either the Anti-Christ or Christ himself is only one opposing extreme among many other contradictory meanings that have been suggested. Is the first rider the personification of human pride and the desire for violent domination, or rather the personification of God's Word and the gospel message? Is he a threatening historical ruler like the Parthian king who rode on a white horse and fought with an arc? Is it the demonic figure of Gog who, according to Ezekiel's prophecies, comes with a bow? Or is it God's angel sent out to protect the faithful and execute God's judgment? From all these contradictory meanings no clear inference can be made, though I tend to see in the first rider the angel of God who comes to protect and to judge.

In whatever way the symbols of the apocalyptic riders are interpreted, they point to the fact that behind the human powers which shape history there are transcendent powers at work which we cannot fully understand. Nevertheless, John's vision gives us one certainty: Christ the Lamb is the one who breaks the seals. The power play on this earth happens in the presence of God, before the eyes of the Christ who has already taken the judgment upon himself and introduced the power of the cross into the course of history. This may also explain why in this cycle of visions, as well as in the following cycles, limits are put to the destructive powers, and the final judgment is delayed (6:6b,8b,11).

In Christian iconography Christ is often represented as the "Agnus Dei", the Lamb of God, holding the cross like a ruler's staff. An early medieval metal relief shows him standing in this position (Fig. c). However, the Christ whom we meet in the sixth chapter of Revelation resembles more the figure on a rare French miniature from the thirteenth century. There Christ appears as a lion with the nimbus around his head, carrying the cross as the sign of his authority (Plate 3). The lion has sharp claws and a fierce look in his eyes. The Latin inscription reads: "You, powerful lion, from the family of David, the tribe of Judah, have risen in glory." Not the sweet little Jesus lamb of romantic piety faces us here, but the apocalyptic Lamb symbolized as the Lion of Judah. He confronts the actors of the political-economic power game and those responsible for the ravages of death with his holy anger.

In that awe-inspiring presence, two groups of people make their appearance. As the fifth and sixth seal of the scroll are opened we hear cries out of the depth. First there are servants of God who have rendered a faithful witness to the power of the Lamb and paid for their testimony with their lives. The blood of sacrificed animals flows to the base of the altar and this is the place where those who, together with Christ, won the victory by becoming victims are thought to reside. Just as the blood of the murdered

Abel cried out from earth to heaven, even so the souls of the witnesses shout from underneath the altar (the soul was considered to reside in the blood). Their cry echoes the complaints of many believers from Old Testament times: "How long, Yahweh?" "From the depths I call to you, Yahweh, Lord, hear my cry!" (Ps. 13 and 130). This cry is heard even today. It is still heard in the screams of those who are tortured for their convictions in prisons and army camps.

More will be said in the next meditation about these witnesses, their number and their attributes. Here it is important to notice that the witnesses are mentioned together with the mighty political and economic powers, even together with death which seems to have the ultimate power. As they make their plea to God, the "holy and true Master", the mad cavalcade of the apocalyptic riders is interrupted. The testimony of those who died for their faith introduces into human awareness the fact of the presence of the Lord of history. It points to the transcendence within our limited time and space. Though seldom acknowledged as such, the prayers of these witnesses have the power to accelerate, or in patience to slow down, the course of history towards its end.

If read in isolation the plea of these witnesses could be taken as a call for personal vengeance. In the context of the whole message of Revelation it is rather a plea that justice be done: God's justice which takes account of the sacrifice of the Lamb while judging all evil powers, God's justice which vindicates the victims and accomplishes the design of salvation.

Only when the world begins to fall apart does another group of people become aware of the divine presence and the anger of the Lamb. The sevenfold enumeration points to all inhabitants of the earth, including the slaves. However, the accent lies on the mighty and powerful who are most tempted to misuse their power against God's will: the kings, the governors, the military commanders, the rich, people of influence among the whole population both slaves and free citizens. Their cry is one of terror, calling to the mountains and rocks: "Fall on us and hide us away from the One who sits on the throne and from the anger of the Lamb. For the Great Day of his anger has come, and who can face it"; literally: "who can stand?"

Who can stand in the presence of the Lord of history? This question is faced in the "Improperia" (= the "Reproaches", "Complaints"), an ancient Christian litany for Good Friday, which goes back to the seventh century. Based on God's "controversy" with this people in the sixth chapter of Micah this litany brings together the saving acts during the exodus with those wrought by Christ's passion. God's people are then challenged to give account of the way in which they responded, and the only response possible is the "Trisagion" and the "Kyrie eleison", the acknowledgment of God's holiness and the plea for forgiveness.

The parallelism between the exodus story and Christ's passion, both pointing to the cost of salvation and the appropriate response of the people, makes this litany a meaningful conclusion for a meditation where we have been reflecting on the anger of the Lamb. There is no cheap grace, no salvation without judgment. During the exodus story the liberating God had to become the judging God. The good news for the oppressed was at least initially bad news for the oppressors. In the second part of the "Improperia" God complains: "For your sake I scourged your captors and their firstborn sons, but you brought your scourges down on me!" "I led you from slavery to freedom and drowned your captors in the sea, but you handed me over to your highpriests." "I opened the sea before you, but you opened my side with a spear."

In the cosmic exodus story of the Book of Revelation the God who sits on the throne again liberates and saves, but in doing so God must destroy what is evil in the churches and in the world. God must shatter the city of Babylon before the New Jerusalem can appear and before all will be made new. There is thus hope, hope for us, for all people, for this universe, but it is not the naive hope of the Western Enlightenment. The biblical message does not promise us gradual progress with only occasional minor setbacks. The hope which John's visions open up for us is one which passes through the fire of judgment. The Lamb who carries the sins of the world is also the Lamb who faces us with a holy anger.

Standing before him who has won the victory by going through the fire of judgment we hear and respond to the complaints of the "Improperia".

Divine voice: *My people, what have I done to you? How have I offended you? Answer me! I led you out of Egypt, from slavery to freedom, but you led your Saviour to the cross. My people, what have I done to you? How have I offended you? Answer me!*

Response:

Divine voice: *For forty years I led you safely through the desert. I fed you with manna from heaven and brought you to a land of plenty; but you led your Saviour to the cross.*

Response: *Agios o Theos.*

Divine voice: *What more could I have done for you?*
I planted you as my fairest vine,
but you yielded only bitterness:
when I was thirsty you gave me vinegar to drink,
and you pierced your Saviour with a lance.

Response: *Agios o Theos.*

4. Salvation to the Lamb

"Wait before you do any damage on land or at sea or to the trees!" World history, on its course to total destruction, is suddenly stopped. At the end of the sixth chapter of Revelation we were in the midst of a cosmic cyclone with the stars falling from heaven, the sun turning black, the sky disappearing and the earth all upside down. Now, at the beginning of the seventh chapter, a divine decree orders that the four winds of the world be held back, that the angels pause before they do their destructive work. Later, John testifies: "The Lamb then broke the seventh seal, and there was silence in heaven for about half an hour" (8:1).

Preparing ourselves for the next vision it is good to keep this cosmic Sabbath rest, to remain silent and then to pray quietly that the Spirit may help us to understand.

(Moment of silence, followed by the repeated singing of "Come Holy Spirit")

Music from Taizé, France

Ve - ni San-cte Spi-ri-tus.

Before world history and the old creation come to an end, the servants of God receive the divine seal on their foreheads, and then we are again lifted up from the earthly scene to stand with the multitude of nations before the throne of God and in front of the Lamb. There we join the choirs of praise:

John: *Next I saw four angels, standing at the four corners of the earth, holding back the four winds of the world to keep them from blowing over the land or the sea or any tree. Then I saw another angel rising where the sun rises, carrying the seal of the living God; he called in a powerful voice to the four angels whose duty was to devastate land and sea:*

Angel: *"Wait before you do any damage on land or at sea or to the trees, until we have put the seal on the foreheads of the servants of our God."*

John: *And I heard how many had been sealed: a hundred and forty-four thousand, out of all the tribes of Israel. From the tribe of Judah, twelve thousand had been sealed; from the tribe of Reuben, twelve thousand; from the tribe of Gad, twelve thousand; from the tribe of Asher, twelve thousand; from the tribe of Naphtali, twelve thousand; from the tribe of Manasseh, twelve thousand; from the tribe of Simeon, twelve thousand; from the tribe of Levi, twelve thousand; from the tribe of Issachar, twelve thousand; from the tribe of Zebulun, twelve thousand; from the tribe of Joseph, twelve thousand; and from the tribe of Benjamin, twelve thousand had been sealed.*

After that I saw that there was a huge number, impossible for anyone to count, of people from every nation, race, tribe and language; they were standing in front of the throne and in front of the Lamb, dressed in white robes and holding palms in their hands. They shouted in a loud voice:

All: *"Salvation to our God*
who sits on the throne,
and to the Lamb!"

John: *And all the angels who were standing in a circle round the throne, surrounding the elders and the four living creatures, prostrated themselves before the throne, and touched the ground with their foreheads, worshipping God with these words:*

All: *"Amen. Praise and glory and wisdom,*
thanksgiving and honour and power and strength
to our God for ever and ever.
Amen."   (7:1-12)

Who are these "servants of God" who receive the seal of the living God? Several Old Testament passages come to one's mind. There is the mark on Cain, a sign of protection which Cain received from God although he had murdered his brother (Gen. 4:15). Circumcision was among the Israelites the main sign of belonging to the covenant people (Gen. 17:9-14), and in the intertestamental Book of the Jubilees it is called a "seal for a day of redemption". In the context of the Book of Revelation another sign of protection is even more strongly recalled: the blood of the Passover lambs placed on the lintel and doorposts of the houses where Israelites lived in Egypt. This sign preserved them from the wrath of God and for the liberation from slavery (Ex. 12:21-23). A fourth allusion made here is to a prophecy of Ezekiel: the sign of the "taw", the cruciform last letter of the Hebrew alphabet, was marked on the forehead of faithful Israelites in Jerusalem. People thus marked were saved from the terrible judgment seen in that vision (Ez. 9:4).

Many Christians will immediately think of their baptism when hearing about the seal of the living God. According to an ancient liturgical practice the sign of the cross is made on the forehead of those who are baptized. Although some New Testament passages on the seal may indirectly allude to baptism, the first text making an explicit relationship between the seal and baptism comes only from post-apostolic times.

Can we then conclude that "the servants of God" are identical with the Jewish people and with the baptized Christians as we know them now? For two reasons this seems to me a dangerous conclusion.

First it must be remembered that in the vision of the seventh chapter John sees God's people from the perspective of heaven. "Heaven" and "earth" do not primarily refer to localities, but to intermingling spheres of influence. "Heaven" is the time and space where God's sovereignty is fully operative, accepted and glorified. The "earth", however, embraces the whole time and space under the dominance and deception of satanic powers. All inhabitants of the earth, including members of the church on earth, are tempted to become worshippers of the beast. This is evident in the passages about the earthly reality of the church made up of Jews and gentiles. Thus the letters to the seven churches in Asia Minor (Rev. 2-3) show that church assemblies here on earth are mixed gatherings consisting of faithful witnesses and the traitors of true faith. In these letters John therefore calls Christians to repentance and encourages them to endure. The seer stands in the tradition of the Old Testament prophets who never tired of warning the Israelites that not all of them belonged to God's people, that only a repentant remnant could serve God's purpose of salvation. John never identifies the earthly church with the servants of God.

Secondly there is the question about the divine "census". The witnesses who had paid their testimony with their lives were told "to be patient a little longer, until the roll was completed of their fellow-servants" (6:11). In the new vision God's servants are marked with the seal of grace and the number hundred and fourty-four thousand is mentioned. This is not the statistical indication for a *numerus clausus* of God's election. The sacred number twelve is squared and multiplied by one thousand. It indicates completeness, fullness, totality. This symbolic number is here applied to the servants coming from the twelve tribes of Israel while later the same number designates the fullness of those who "follow the Lamb wherever he goes" (14:1,4). This divinely ordered election and setting apart of God's servants stand in a striking contrast to the census which king David once conducted. He was tempted to find out and calculate the strength of his military power (2 Sam. 24:1-10), an arrogance immediately punished. This is a healthy warning for Christians who want to know exactly who is inside or outside the holy company, how many are the elect. They follow human statistics and not God's arithmetic where numbers have a qualitative rather than a quantitative meaning. True growth is measured more according to maturity than according to numbers. A mature minority can indeed serve the divine purpose better than an immature majority. Our vocation is to persevere as witnesses, not to make a census and to count the number of God's servants.

What John received in his vision is a glimpse of how *God* sees his servants. Two groups are mentioned together, first the totality of servants from the twelve tribes of Israel and then the "huge number, impossible for anyone to count, of people from every nation, race, tribe and language". Exegetes have puzzled over this twofold crowd. Do they refer to the celestial assembly of faithful by distinguishing between those coming from among Jews and gentiles? Is the first group the militant church here on earth while the second group represents all those who completed already their testimony and who now worship before God's throne? Does the twofold enumeration point to one and the same assembly of God's servants, first from an Old Testament perspective and then from a New Testament point of view? Or are the two groups the remnant of the people of Israel and the remnant of the church from all nations as God sees and restores them? In the light of the fact that the whole of John's Revelation is strongly built on the affirmations of faith in the Old Testament, this last-mentioned option seems to me the most probable one. Moses is explicitly called a "servant of God" (15:3). Even in the New Jerusalem the names of "the twelve tribes of Israel" are inscribed over the twelve gates, while its twelve foundation stones carry the names of "the twelve apostles of the Lamb" (21:12,14).

What is the vocation of this twofold assembly of God's servants? In heaven it consists of worship. John sees them "standing in front of the throne and in front of the Lamb, dressed in white robes and holding palms in their hands", joining the praise of the heavenly host. The worship is described with symbols and expressions recalling the joyful Jewish pilgrim festival of the "sukkôt". During this eight-day feast of the tabernacles the Israelites remember the desert journey after the exodus by living in temporary huts. The waving of palm branches accompanied the singing of psalms during the processions in the temple court. Especially the call "Hosanna!" from Psalm 118:25 played an important role. It was originally a plea for help: "Yahweh, save us!" but soon it became also a joyful acclamation: "Salvation to you, Yahweh!"

During his entry into Jerusalem on Palm Sunday Jesus was received with this plea and acclamation. The Gospel of John reports how a great crowd of people "took branches of palm and went out to receive Jesus, shouting: 'Hosanna! Blessed is he who is coming in the name of the Lord, the king of Israel'" (John 12:13). This welcome of the earthly Jesus on his way to the cross is transposed into the heavenly liturgy. Here the plea and acclamation are addressed to God and to Christ the Lamb.

A Spanish miniature from the eleventh century shows the heavenly "sukkôt" feast (Plate 4). It comes from an illuminated manuscript of the famous commentary on Revelation written by the monk Beatus. In the eighth century he had escaped from Muslim-occupied Spain and found refuge in the small Christian kingdom of Asturia, the mountainous part of Northern Spain. During the following centuries Asturian Christians not only studied and copied the learned commentary of Beatus, but they illuminated it with some of the most striking miniatures produced in the European Middle Ages. In fact, the Book of Revelation became for them *the* Bible, the central testimony to Jesus Christ. Their visual interpretation of John's vision can still speak to us.

The vocation of God's servants in heaven consists of worship. As the sphere of heaven extends to the earth, worship is the centre of the servants' vocation here on earth as well. However, because the earth has become the sphere of demonic powers, God's witnesses are involved on earth in a struggle, leading to suffering and often to death. Therefore John's Revelation is often characterized as a book for martyrs. This designation can be misleading. The Greek terms *martys*="witness" and *martyrion*= "testimony" have in the Book of Revelation not yet the specific martyriological significance which they received later in the early church. It is not the death for Christ's sake which constitutes the testimony asked of God's servants, though their testimony often leads to violent death (6:9). According to John's visions the vocation of God's servants here on earth is to worship, and to be witnesses of God's Word, of God's judging and saving presence in world history. They are called "to be the first fruits for God and for the Lamb" (14:4), to let the powers of heaven become operative here on earth. What counts is not the personal piety of the witness sealed by martyrdom but the truth of God's Word and promise, testified among the nations. The twofold company of God's servants thus has not primarily been elected for their own salvation by a martyr's death, but for the vocation of worship and costly witness.

This corresponds to the main biblical passages which speak about election. God chooses God's servant people with a view to mission. Abraham was thus elected to become a blessing among all the clans of the earth (Gen. 12:1-3). The Servant of God in the prophecies of the Second Isaiah was chosen to become a light to the nations (Isa. 42:6). The exodus story leads to its climax when at

Sinai God meets with some Israelite tribes and constitutes
them as his own people to be a "kingdom of priests" (Ex.
19:6). Whatever that may originally have meant — the
role of priests changed considerably in subsequent periods
of the Old Testament — after the exile the priestly
function was mainly linked with sacrificial worship. Early
Christians, especially the author of the letter to the
Hebrews, saw the passion of Christ as a radical
reinterpretation of the priestly function. According to the
pattern laid down by the priesthood of Christ, to be a
priest now meant to offer oneself for God's purpose,
becoming thus part of the one perpetual offering of praise
and witness made by Christ.

It is significant that three out of the four New Testament
references to Exodus 19:6 are found in the cosmic exodus
story of Revelation (1:6; 5:10; 20:6). The priestly function
assigned to the servants of God forbids them to abandon
the world of nations in its course towards death and
destruction. They must witness to the Lamb who by his
sacrifice took away the sins of the *world* and their
testimony concerns therefore God's purpose of salvation
for the whole creation. This testimony they can give only
according to the pattern pioneered by Christ's priesthood:
the priest becoming victim.

During the liturgy of John's vision in the seventh
chapter of Revelation the heavenly host does not sing:
"Salvation to the world!" Instead we hear the strange plea
and acclamation: "Salvation to our God and to the Lamb!"
Do God and the Lamb need to be saved? This text has
given considerable difficulty to translators. The Good
News Bible renders the passage with the words:
"Salvation comes from our God and from the Lamb." This
certainly is true, but it does not correspond to the original
text. The New English Bible comes nearer to the original
by translating: "Victory to our God and to the Lamb."
Nevertheless, whether this fits our concept of God or not,

the original version does indeed state: "*Salvation* to our God and to the Lamb!"

The precarious situation of Christian witnesses in Asia Minor towards the end of the first century can throw some light on this strange prayer. From 81 to 96 A.D. Domitian ruled as an absolute lord. He was the first Roman emperor who claimed to be divine and demanded that he be worshipped as "God the Lord". Coins were issued under his reign which show Domitian as Zeus, the supreme god. When in the year 88 a conspiracy against the emperor had been cruelly crushed, a coin of celebration was struck with the inscription: "For the deliverance of him who is worthy of all adoration." Another inscription from Asia Minor carries the following doxology: "To Zeus the Supreme, the Saviour, the Emperor Domitian." In Ephesus a provincial sanctuary for the worship of Domitian was erected. Celebrations of the imperial cult in that city included solemn processions, games with liturgical acclamations, with miraculous sound and light effects, with spectacular races, battles, tortures, executions — all to the greater glory of the image of Domitian, enthroned on the throne of the gods.

In this situation the small minority of Christians began to wonder. They had made God's cause their own, yet all around them people proclaimed that Domitian was the saviour. By all human standards Caesar and not Christ the Lamb had wrought the victory. Anxious thoughts and doubts thus arose in the hearts of those Christians, doubts which until today have assailed believers as God's cause is contested and ridiculed. Is the hope for a new heaven and a new earth simply a wishful dream? There are so many dreams! Is the ultimate victory really that of Christ, the Lion of Judah who became the slaughtered Lamb?

Belief in God is no longer either a matter of course or a thing of little import for witnesses who, because of their testimony, risk violent death. It becomes a matter of life or death. What is at stake for them is not any longer their own predicament, the outcome of this or that earthly struggle, not even their own salvation. The only matter which counts for them is whether or not God exists, whether God's purpose of salvation will be realized or not. Like great gamblers the servants of God either quit the game or put all their stakes on the triple conviction: (1) that Christ's death and resurrection was indeed the decisive victory which has cosmic repercussions; (2) that "heaven", God's judging and saving presence, penetrates this earth; and (3) that the all-embracing peace will dawn when God creates all things new.

All this is implied in the shout of "Hosanna!" — "Salvation to God and to the Lamb!" God's servants in heaven sing it as an affirmation of faith with full confidence. Here on earth we still pray it as a plea, often with wavering faith, full of hesitations and doubts. In the heavenly liturgy the "Hosanna!" is immediately followed by a sevenfold praise, assigning to God "praise and glory and wisdom, thanksgiving and honour and power and strength". No more radical cure for our little faith exists than to join the multitudes from every nation, race, tribe and language in their mighty song of praise:

Psalm 117:1   Music from Taizé, France

Lau-da - te om-nes gen-tes, lau - da - te Do-mi - num. Lau-
da - te om-nes gen - tes, lau - da - te Do-mi - num!

All peoples, praise the Lord!

5. The Marriage Feast of the Shepherd-Lamb

Music from Taizé, France

Ho - san - na, ho - san - na, ho - san - na in ex - cel - sis.

Called as we are to worship and costly witness, we confess together with Christ's church of all ages and continents:

We believe in one Lord, Jesus Christ,
the only Son of God,
eternally begotten of the Father
Light from Light,
true God from true God,
begotten, not made,
of one Being with the Father:
through him all things were made.
For us and for our salvation he came down from
*   heaven;*
by the power of the Holy Spirit he became incarnate
from the Virgin Mary
he was made man.
For our sake he was crucified under Pontius Pilate;
he suffered death and was buried;
on the third day he rose again in accordance with
*   the scriptures;*
he ascended into heaven.
He is seated at the right hand of the Father,
he will come again in glory
to judge the living and the dead,
and his kingdom will have no end.

The above confession to Christ is the central part of the most widely accepted creed in the church universal: the final version of the Nicene Creed as it was accepted in 451 A.D. by the Fourth Ecumenical Council meeting in Chalcedon. It is revealing to compare this fourth- and fifth-century confession of faith with the witness to Christ found in the Book of Revelation.

Both the church fathers and John the seer strongly emphasize the intimate union between God the Father and Christ the Son. According to the Revelation the two rule together, although only the Father is called the "Lord God" and the "Almighty" ("Pantocrator"). Otherwise many attributes given to God are also conferred on Christ: he is the "Holy" and the "Trustworthy One", the "Alpha and the Omega", especially the "Living One". Together God and the Lamb receive the same liturgical acclamations (though after the seventh chapter these hymns are addressed only to God). In the New Jerusalem God and the Lamb together replace the temple with its altar, and the splendour of their glory makes the light of the sun and the moon redundant. It is from their throne that the river of living water issues. While according to the creed Christ "is seated at the right hand of the Father", in John's visions the Lamb sits together with God on the throne, even "at the heart of the throne".

The church fathers used both biblical and Greek philosophical terms, which came out of the early church's doctrinal discussions, for describing who Christ is. Among the rich variety of designations for Christ in John's visions several are not found anywhere in the New Testament except in the Book of Revelation; for instance the "faithful witness", the "bright star from the morning" and especially the "Lamb" (*arnion*). Others have New Testament parallels such as the classic titles "Son of Man", "Christ" and "Son of God", but also the descriptions of Jesus as the "First-born of the dead", the "Principle of God's creation", the "Word of God", the "Lord of lords and King of kings". Almost all these attributes are strongly rooted in the Old Testament. This is especially true for the passages where Jesus is described as the "highest of earthly kings", the "Amen", the one who "has the key of David", the "Lion of Judah", the "Root of David", the one who "tests motives and thoughts", the "first and the last". John witnesses to Christ's revealing and saving work according to the pattern of God's work described in the Psalms and by Old Testament prophets, foremost among them Isaiah, especially the Second Isaiah, but also Jeremiah, Ezekiel, and Daniel. Sometimes the work of the personified Wisdom in the post-exilic wisdom literature is recalled.

When confessing Christ the church fathers and John the seer look both backwards and forwards. From God's point of view they see after the creation world history moving from one focal point of an ellipse to the other. The first concerns the coming of the Christ into this world in the person of Jesus. The second points to the future return of Christ and the completion of God's plan of salvation.

In recalling the decisive past accomplishments both the church fathers and John concentrate on the birth, passion, resurrection and ascension, without explicit references to the earthly life and teaching of Jesus. The creed enumerates the sequence of events, rooting them firmly in human history ("crucified under Pontius Pilate") with only one general reference to "the Scriptures". In the Revelation a symbolic-theological interpretation of the past saving acts is given with a great wealth of Old Testament allusions: for the birth of Christ in the twelfth chapter and for the far more strongly emphasized passion and resurrection by the figure of Christ the Lamb.

Looking forward to the coming work of Christ the creed affirms: "He will come again in glory to judge the living and the dead, and his kingdom will have no end." John also confesses that Christ comes again, but he does so with much greater urgency than the church fathers. For him the final cataclysm is imminent. At the very beginning he warns the readers: "The Time is near!" At the end Jesus himself affirms: "I am indeed coming soon!" (1:3; 22:20). The Apocalypse therefore appropriately concludes with the appeal: "Come, Lord Jesus!", the early Christian liturgical shout "Maranatha" (22:20; 1 Cor. 16:22).

Many of our contemporaries feel, like John, that cosmic catastrophes are threatening today and that we live in apocalyptic times. The danger at such times is that we may become so fascinated or so frightened by this coming end that the first focal point of history is lost sight of, namely the decisive victory already won. John always kept the past and the future focus of world history together. We must learn from him to do so in the midst of the threatening cataclysms of today.

Does the Christ of the Apocalypse come to judge the living and the dead? The answer is less obvious than one usually assumes. True, Christians are accountable to Christ for the testimony which they render (cp. the letters to the seven churches). It is also the Lamb who opens the seals of the scroll and thus unleashes the cavalcade of apocalyptic riders. However, if one examines the eighteen passages in Revelation which use explicit judgment terminology (*krinein*, *krima*, *krisis*, *ekdikein*), sixteen refer directly or indirectly to God (e.g. 6:10; 18:8ff.; 20:11ff.). Once the power of judgment is given to an unidentified group (20:4). The Lamb never appears as the judge, and only once — in the fearful description of Christ's return (19:11-21) — it is stated that "in uprightness he judges and makes war". Old Testament images of God's judging activity are there transferred to Christ (Ps. 2:9; Isa. 63:1ff.).

Read in isolation this passage indeed describes an almost unbearable judgment scene in which Christ, his cloak soaked in blood, smites the nations with his sharp sword. However, several details in the text itself allow another understanding of Christ's function in God's judgment. "Trustworthy and true", "known by the name 'the Word of God'", Christ judges and makes war in a totally different way than the beast and the kings of the earth do. The Lion of Judah has become the sacrificed Lamb. The blood soaking his cloak is his own and not that of his enemies. He has taken God's judgment upon himself. The sword issuing from his mouth is his testimony which confounds the demonic powers. This explains why the expected final battle does not take place when Christ with the armies of heaven and the beast with the armies of the kings of the earth confront each other. Without any struggle the beast is imprisoned. Contrary to what is confessed in the creed, the Christ of the Apocalypse will not primarily come to judge the living and the dead. He comes as the witness in the cosmic court, as the trial goes on between God and creation, witnessing for God's faithful servants and against those who worshipped the beast, inside and outside the church.

The creed says little about the present work of Christ: "He is seated at the right hand of the Father." John's visions emphasize the presence of the risen Lord much more. Much of the work which the creed assigns to the Holy Spirit the Revelation assigns to Christ the Lamb. "I am the Living One, I was dead and look — I am alive for ever and ever" (1:18). This presence and communion of Christ with God's servants is paradoxically described as that of the Shepherd-Lamb with his sheep. Later the image of a bridegroom with his bride is used. The presence of the Lamb thus leads to a feast. In John's vision of the seventh chapter we meet the Shepherd-Lamb and in the conclusion of all the visions before the return of Christ we are invited to the Lamb's marriage feast (19:1-10).

John: *One of the elders then spoke and asked me:*
Elder: *"Who are these people, dressed in white robes, and where have they come from?"*

John: *I answered him: "You can tell me, sir." Then he said:*

Elder: *"These are the people who have been through the great trial; they have washed their robes white again in the blood of the Lamb. That is why they are standing in front of God's throne and serving him day and night in his sanctuary; and the One who sits on the throne will spread his tent over them. They will never hunger or thirst again; sun and scorching wind will never plague them, because the Lamb who is at the heart of the throne will be their shepherd and will guide them to springs of living water; and God will wipe away all tears from their eyes."*

(7:13-17)

John: *Then a voice came from the throne; it said:*

Voice: *"Praise our God, you servants of his and those who fear him, small and great alike."*

John: *And I heard what seemed to be the voices of a huge crowd, like the sound of the ocean or the great roar of thunder, answering:*

All: *"Alleluia! The reign of the Lord our God Almighty has begun; let us be glad and joyful and give glory to God, because this is the time for the marriage of the Lamb. His bride is ready, and she has been able to dress herself in dazzling white linen, because her linen is made of the good deeds of the saints."*

John: *The angel said:*

Angel: *"Write this: 'Blessed are those who are invited to the wedding feast of the Lamb.'"*

(19:5-9)

The worshipping assembly of the servants of God who were marked on their foreheads with the divine seal are here described as "the people who have been through the great trial; they have washed their robes white again in the blood of the Lamb" (7:14). A daring image: to wash white in the red blood! They stand before God's throne because they accepted what Christ has done for us: "He loves us and has washed away our sins with his blood" (1:5). They became witnesses to Christ, the Lion of Judah who as the Lamb was slaughtered and sacrificed, who with his blood "bought people for God" (5:9). Therefore they had to go through great trial and tribulation.

John sees in his visions much blood flowing, too much for my liking. However, in the twelve places where blood is mentioned in the Book of Revelation it never refers explicitly to the blood of enemies (unless the winepress image from Isa. 63:1ff. in Rev. 14:20 is understood as such and related to the appearance of Christ in 19:13). The blood which John sees flowing is either a symbol of judgment — e.g. "the moon turned red as blood" — or it explicitly refers to the blood shed by the Lamb and the witnesses of the Lamb. To see what John saw and to hear what he heard means to face the hard realities of Christ's passion and the suffering of God's servants, including the reality of shed blood known to many of our fellow human beings today.

Nevertheless, persecutions and suffering, judgment and blood are not the last words of the Apocalypse. Christ the Passover Lamb and the Suffering Servant is also the Shepherd who guides his witnesses to the living water. Two prophecies from Ezekiel must have been in the mind of John: God's promise that a new David will come to shepherd his people and the vision of the new temple from which issues a river of living water to let grow abundant life (Ezek. 34:23; 47:1-12).

A twelfth-century engraving on a gilded copper plate shows the Shepherd Lamb not only as the guide on the way to the living water, but as the spring from which the life-giving water issues into all the world (Plate 5). Upright the victorious Lamb stands on the mountain of Paradise. Around him the circular Latin inscription indicates what led to this cosmic message of life: "Becoming a sacrifice this holy Lamb has taken away the sins." The blood which flows from the Lamb becomes the life-giving rivers of Paradise: Gyon and Phison, Tigris and Euphrates, whose names are inscribed on the borders above and below and whom the medieval artist portrayed as personified springs of water. The text on the two side margins announces that the four rivers of Paradise flow from Christ and are carried into all the world.

By showing the cosmic extension of the work of Christ the artist went beyond John's vision about the Shepherd Lamb. However, this vision itself already anticipates the larger vision in the last two chapters of Revelation. There God will spread his tent not only over his servants but over all human beings, his peoples (the same verb is used in 7:15 and in 21:3 where the better attested text has the plural "his peoples" and not the singular "his people"). In the new creation all tears will be wiped away, not only those of Christ's witnesses. All will have access to the water of life, for all will then be made new. The nations will come into the New Jerusalem whose gates are never closed, for there will be no more darkness nor anything accursed. The river of living water will flow from the throne of God and the Lamb, giving abundant growth to the trees of life whose leaves are for the healing of the nations (21:5f., 24f.; 22:1-3).

In this final vision the intimate communion between the Lamb and the New Jerusalem is compared to the relationship of a bridegroom with his bride (21:2,9; 22:17). Old Testament prophets had already used the image of marriage for speaking about God's covenant with God's people. In a few passages in the Gospels and Paul's letters Christ is pictured as the bridegroom for his church, and the marriage feast occasionally becomes a parable for the future messianic meal in God's kingdom.

Most explicitly this imagery is used in the last hymnic passage of the Book of Revelation (19:1-10), part of which we recited earlier.

The first hymns (19:1-4) with their threefold "Alleluia" are juxtaposed with the moving laments about the destruction of the great city of Babylon, which symbolizes not only Rome but all human societies which are blind to God's presence and therefore worship idols, persecuting the prophets of God and witnesses of the Lamb (18:1-24). These hymns are sung by a large crowd in heaven together with the elders and the four living creatures. They once again confess that God's judgments are true and just.

Then, in Revelation 19:5, a new call to worship is heard. This time the servants of God are addressed, but no indication is given where this second part of the liturgy takes place. Does it already anticipate the worship of the whole new creation when there will be a new heaven and a new earth? The response to the call is overwhelming, like the sound of the ocean or the great roar of thunder: "Alleluia!", the huge crowd sings, "the reign of the Lord our God Almighty has begun; let us be glad and joyful and give glory to God, because this is the time for the marriage of the Lamb!"

Again one wonders who belong to this great crowd and who is the bride of the Lamb. Most commentators identify them with the Christian church. However, in the final vision the bride clearly appears as the personified New Jerusalem. Undoubtedly the servants of God, often associated or identified with the "saints" and the "witnesses of Jesus", play an important role within this crowd and within the New Jerusalem. It is they who will see God and the Lamb "face to face, and his name will be written on their foreheads" (22:4). But these chosen ones who follow the Lamb wherever he goes are called to be an *aparchē*, "the first fruits for God and the Lamb" (14:4). By their costly witness they confess now already the one whom all will see, "even those who pierced him" (1:7). In their worship they anticipate the cosmic worship of the new creation.

Three things are indicated in this passage concerning the bride:

— She must be ready. John's Revelation is like a trumpet call which awakes those who are asleep in the midst of the cataclysms of world history, those who are misled by the tricks of satanic powers.

— The bride does not make her dazzling white marriage dress herself but she receives it. The original text insists on the fact that the dress is *given* to her.

— Nevertheless, the readiness of the bride for the marriage is related to what the saints, the servants of God, do. The Greek term designating these deeds (*dikaiōma*) is difficult to translate. In the song of the Lamb, the only other text where in the Book of Revelation the same word appears, *dikaiōma* is translated with "acts of saving justice" (15:4).

What John saw and heard is a warning and an encouragement. Now we can add that it is also an invitation to celebrate: "Blessed are those who are invited to the wedding feast of the Lamb!"

This series of meditations can therefore best end with a festive meal and the celebration of the Lord's Supper. The eucharistic liturgy must reflect the mood of the Revelation:

— a worship which squarely faces the evil forces and the suffering in this world;

— a worship where the ancient liturgical hymns and shouts receive in the light of John's Revelation a new meaning: the "Sanctus", the "Gloria", the "Agnus Dei", the "Hosanna", the "Maranatha" and the "Amen";

— a counter-worship against the idolatries of our time;

— a worship which, despite our doubts and discouragement, becomes expectant and joyful, where the "Alleluia" sets the tone:

Pablo Sosa, Argentina

1. El cielo canta alegría, ¡Aleluya! por que en tu vida y la mía brilla la gloria de Dios. ¡Aleluya, Aleluya, Aleluya, Aleluya, Aleluya!
1. Heaven is singing for joy, Alleluia! for in your life and mine is shining the glory of God. Alleluia, Alleluia, Alleluia, Alleluia, Alleluia!

2. El cielo canta alegría, ¡Aleluya! / porque a tu vida y la mía las une el amor de Dios.
3. El cielo canta alegría, ¡Aleluya! / porque tu vida y la mía proclamarán al Señor.

2. Heaven is singing for joy, Alleluia! / for your life and mine are one in the love of God.
3. Heaven is singing for joy, Alleluia! / for your life and mine will always proclaim the Lord.

In such a festive worship an abstract sermon has no place. The seer John communicates, like an artist, mainly with images. The sixth-century mosaics in the sanctuary of San Vitale in Ravenna recount many of the visions which John has seen (Plate 6).

In the apse we see Jesus holding in his hand the still-sealed scroll. He sits on the sphere of the cosmos, his feet on the mountain of Paradise. The angel on his right leads to him Vitalis, the patron saint of the church to whom Christ tends the crown of martyrs. To his left another angel leads Ecclesius into Christ's presence, the person who commissioned the church and who carries a model of the building. Above the youthful Christ hover the clouds of divine majesty. On the arch of the apse appear two eagles, ancient symbols of light and power who in Roman art often carry a medallion with the emperor's image.

Here this image is replaced by the Christ monogram in a
circle. The arch is adorned with many horns of plenty,
symbols of abundant life. Under the windows on the wall
of the apse the stylized buildings on the two sides
represent Jerusalem and Bethlehem as symbols of the
church gathered out of Jews and gentiles. In the middle
two angels carry a sign of light. Our attention is then
drawn upwards to the windows surrounded by vine
branches with doves who symbolize the blessed ones in
Paradise. Then, almost inevitably our eyes are lifted still
higher to the zenith of the dome, focusing on the Lamb
who stands upright and looks at us.

If we view the two side walls we see there the large
portrayals of two Old Testament sacrificial scenes. On the
left the three angels visit Abraham in Mamre to announce
the birth of Isaac. The patriarch brings to them the roasted
calf, carrying it as a priest holds the host. No more fully
visible on the reproduction is the subsequent scene, with
Abraham ready to sacrifice Isaac. The mosaic to the right
shows a large altar with Abel on one side and the priest-
king Melchizedek on the other making their sacrifices.
Above the arcs angels present the cross with its precious
stones. On the wall we see the prophet Isaiah to the right
and the prophet Jeremiah to the left. The two scenes near
the apse are both taken from the exodus story. On the right
side the youthful Moses is portrayed and above him God's
meeting with Moses at the burning bush. On the left side
we see the waiting Israelites while above them Moses
receives God's will and promise on Mount Sinai. Again
our eyes are lifted up to the four evangelists and still
higher up to the Lamb at the zenith.

If finally we look up to the arch above the entry of the
sanctuary we notice the medallions with busts of the
apostles leading upwards to Peter and Paul with the risen
Christ in their midst. The medallions are held by dolphins,
symbols of life and power. From there once more our eyes

are drawn up to the dome. In the four corners peacocks stand on spheres which are placed on platforms supported by dolphins. With their wheel of plumes the peacocks act as the carriers of heaven, the eyes on the plumes representing the stars. Four garlands made of laurels, tokens of immortality and fame, lead to the crown of laurels. The triangular areas of the dome are filled with acanthus leaves, with fruit and birds, all symbols of the tree of life. Four angels hold up the crown and in their midst stands the Lamb with the nimbus. He no longer carries the cross, but stands waiting among the stars for those who are invited to his wedding feast.

Like much in Byzantine art these mosaics of Ravenna are in danger of verging on triumphalism. Those who read the Book of Revelation face the same danger. It is necessary therefore to remember that the Lamb in the dome of San Vitale stands immediately above the altar and that the church is dedicated to a Christian martyr. The Lamb to whose wedding feast we are invited went on his way to the cross. It is this Christ whom we meet if we respond to the invitation.

"Blessed are those who are invited to the wedding feast of the Lamb!"

Acknowledgments

The Bible translation used in these meditations is that of *The New Jerusalem Bible* (London, 1985) by permission of Darton, Longman & Todd (for the USA, Canada and the Philippines: Doubleday & Co., New York). This translation was chosen because it lends itself for liturgical celebrations. Occasionally a more literal rendering of the Greek text has been added in brackets and, contrary to that version, the term *orgē* is translated not by "retribution" but with "anger" while *thymos* is rendered by "fury".

There is a wealth of commentaries and detailed exegetical studies on John's Revelation. I am deeply thankful to the authors of many of these publications, some of whom have spent their whole life examining and meditating on the last book of the Bible. I am especially indebted to those scholars who wrote about the Christ of the Apocalypse and the liturgical background of John's visions. A good up-to-date bibliography is to be found in U.B. Müller's concise commentary *Die Offenbarung des Johannes* (Gütersloh/Würzburg, 1984). Those who want to pursue the study of the Apocalypse can best begin by reading the whole Revelation in several translations before turning to the often contradictory results of scholarly research. A popular self-study guide with questions and helpful short comments has just been published which also gives a short annotated bibliography of recent commentaries and studies in English: T. Grimsrud, *The Triumph of the Lamb* (Scottdale, Pa./Kitchener, Ont., 1987). An excellent pastoral exposition of the message of John's Revelation is D. Mollat, *Une lecture pour aujourd'hui: l'Apocalypse* (Paris, 1982).

For meditation on the Book of Revelation, text analysis and cognitive understanding are not enough. The media of poetry and stories, visual art and music are equally important. Therefore I would recommend as a good companion reading to the Apocalypse the first and the last books in the series *Chronicles of Narnia* (Penguin Books, 1950-56) where C.S. Lewis retells the story of John's Revelation for children and all those who would approach it like children.

This is only one among many literary transpositions of the Apocalypse by writers and poets. For many other examples see the commentary of Ch. Brütsch, *La Clarté de l'Apocalypse* (Geneva, 1966⁵).

The reproductions of visual art on John's Revelation in this booklet are published with the permission of the following copyright holders:

Plate 1: Ivory tablet called Nicasius Diptychon, Tournai Cathedral, Institut royal du patrimoine artistique, Bruxelles, Belgium.

Plate 2: Vivian Bible, MS Latin I, fol. 415 v°, Archives photographiques, Bibliothèque nationale, Paris, France.

Plate 3: Liber floridus, Lat. 8865 f 43, Archives photographiques, Bibliothèque nationale, Paris, France.

Plate 4: Burgo de Osma, Codex 1, folio 92v, Editions Zodiaque, La Pierre qui Vire, France.

Plate 5: The Lamb and the Rivers of Living Water, Inventory No. Cl 1326, cliché des Musées nationaux, Paris, France.

Plate 6: Mosaic in the sanctuary of San Vitale, Deutsches archäologisches Institut, Rome, No. 57-1805.

The line drawings of figures a-c were made after photographs of the original art work reproduced in G. Schiller, *Ikonographie der christlichen Kunst*, Vol. II and III (Gütersloh, 1968 and 1986²), reproductions II, 406; III, 424, 545.

All reproduced art work is analyzed in these two volumes of G. Schiller, except Plate 4 which is discussed in H. Stierlin, *Le livre de feu: l'Apocalypse dans l'Art Mozarabe* (Geneva, 1980). Ch. Brütsch, *op. cit.*, makes many references to artistic interpretations and devotes an appendix to "The Apocalypse in Art" (pp.442-449; bibliography pp.491f.). Also P. Minear, *I Saw a New Earth: an Introduction to the Visions of the Apocalypse* (Washington/ Cleveland, 1968) is very sensitive with regard to the relationship between the Revelation and the arts (bibliography on pp.69f., 128f., 197). A representative collection of modern visual art on the Apocalypse is reproduced and discussed by R.W. Gasser and B. Holeczek (eds), *Apokalypse: ein Prinzip der Hoffnung?* (Heidelberg, 1985). For the iconography of the Lamb see the article

"Lamm, Lamm Gottes" in E. Kirschbaum (ed), *Lexikon der christlichen Ikonographie* (Rome/Freiburg etc., 1968-1976, Vol.III, pp.7-14) and G. Schiller, *op. cit.*, II, pp.129-133 and III, pp.283-303.

The hymns and music in this booklet are printed by permission of the copyright holders:

— p. 1: Per Harling, Stockholm, Sweden;
— p. 11: Grandchamp Community, Areuse, Switzerland;
— p. 22: Hampton Institute Press, Hampton, VA, USA.
— p. 31: Orthodox Liturgy, USSR;
— pp. 33, 42 and 43: composer: J. Berthier. © Ateliers et Presses de Taizé, 71250 Taizé-Communauté, France. Also: GIA, Chicago, and Collins, London;
— p. 53: Pablo Sosa, Buenos Aires, Argentina;

On the whole composers were less sensitive to the hymnic character of the Book of Revelation than visual artists to its symbolic-visionary character. J.H. Cone, *The Spirituals and the Blues* (New York, 1972, pp.86-107) discusses the role of heaven and judgment in Black Spirituals strongly influenced by the Apocalypse. Ch. Brütsch, *op. cit.*, lists hymns and larger musical compositions (cantatas and oratorios) inspired by parts or the whole of John's Revelation (pp.433 and 446f.). For the twentieth century one should add works like William Walton's "Belshazzar's Feast" (1931) and Vaughan Williams' "Sancta Civitas" (1926).